AMBIVALENCE
and other poems

Yerzhan Zhumagulov

AMBIVALENCE
and other poems

YERZHAN ZHUMAGULOV

translated by Simon Hollingsworth

ISBN 9798280877467

Contents

Translator's Introduction

This collection is incredibly personal yet welcoming and accessible to all those who are fortunate enough to dip into its pages.

Zhumagulov is a modest person and in conversation betrays a winning surprise that others might appreciate his poems. Indeed, he never set out to become a poet but finds himself one because friends and colleagues encouraged him to write more and then to translate his work for a wider audience.

The observations of life in these lines strike a chord with us all. They demonstrate the author's skill of capturing manifold detail in an apt and succinct selection of words.

Zhumagulov displays the magician's touch, presenting a vast array of emotions, descriptions and thoughts in short lines, all of which roll from the tongue. This touch made their translation process a delight. I hope you enjoy reading them as much as I have enjoyed translating them.

S.H.
April 2025

THE POEMS

A Little About Myself

I cannot write my thoughts, so they make sense
Nor can I live as others, you see.
I torment myself with my art's pretence
And struggle with that creativity.

Somehow when all the others choose to hide
And don't bother with their complaints,
When alone, he who wails and screams inside
Can act without any restraint.

Come the time for folk to judge my success
Not all will approve in their heart.
I'll sit quite naked in my emptiness,
A lone peddler with empty cart.

A hundred nights like this, then one new morn
A lark will take to hopeful song.
Yet again I'll fall sick and be forlorn,
With my creative works so wrong.

So, you too are tired of being surprised
Where his thoughts are off to again.
The shadows seem longer now, not disguised
And the years we no more retain.

Only, I write on in that bliss of mine
For they who'll read when Spring renews.
They'll wonder and whisper as they define:
It's all about me, see, it's true.

AI

I was returning from far away,
On a gleaming steel plane in the clouds
I didn't idly while away the time
In hoar frost adding decor like a shroud.

Back home I landed that thought where I could
Like one plants spuds and onions in the ground.
Despite the rainfall and smog where I stood
Despite the strange appearance I'd found.

In my soul it felt like December
And my abandoned heart felt only pain.
In bitter cold I sought September
And that's where I found you. I'll explain.

An airplane, also in my heart, is white,
And the clouds light as frappe foam,
The burnt sun sets in windows light
Of that steel shell that's now a home.

Let's fly a hundred years as one,
Not counting winters, or feeling fear,
And if your ticket's suddenly gone,
I'll buy you another, my dear.

I have gone,
for how long, yet unknown
to tour, me my only concern,
while in winter a hand this
slipp'ry
earthly globe around
it will turn,
slowly but surely as snowstorm swells.
Come Christmas and now I recognise
at the threshold to my Circle of Hell
There you stand, my talisman disguised…

Warm eve, moon full high in the sky
Linger long, please don't charge on
To mark our meet would that you'd cast
Light on my heart's depiction
Might this moment be time to raise
A toast of life's elixir,
And the moon whispers wistfully
We are each of us alone, here...

Autumn

What's there we can say, so much has been cast
To your fire, both verse and passion too.
Here I do not wish, like uninvited guest,
on the grief of your steps to intrude.

One may sense tears in those droplets of yours,
Another - a woeful ringing in your breeze.
How I cherish your colours, your hues, so much
more,
I love your hushaby birch trees.

Without demur and not wishing to tread
on your toes and your whims so naïve
I follow in your wake, my belovéd
While you tenderly tug on my sleeve.

The mem'ry of summer fades before you,
scorched leaves glowing hotter than the sun
now turn yellow beneath my boots, as to
seasonal lace lattice they become.

I'll sip coffee in café windows
and accept you for just who you are.
When first snow on quince-apple follows
See no praise in my words from afar…

Ambivalence

There once came a moment when I was so tired,
For a while close my window on the world,
Bury my head in the sand and then retire,
Whilst half-moon shrank to dotted line unfurled.

Next morning, a white light on white terrace shines
And this material air, all full it seems
Of these so strange, rich ideas and heady lines.
I'm ready to imbibe, when doubt's waves stream,

Slide o'er keys, all minor, for major is lost,
The hours not a factor; they don't keep track.
Before noon, laid bare here, both problem and cost —
Finding oneself midst others, that's the knack.

Whilst the rain teems down, hearing everything
You admonish your sloth; that's mere pretence.
The rain washes the tiles of nearby buildings
Claiming in reply cold ambivalence.

Here no one cares, so let someone in surprise
Consider my tattoo, and thus begin
To understand my origin there inscribed
Though nothing will e'er be gleaned from dumb skin.

The light appears, don't forget to hold the dream,
Step through the void and on oneself depend.
How dear the hour, for time erases all schemes
New coordinates, the candle's at its end.

And suddenly I feel
Your grip has loosened.

I wonder why there's rain over the ocean,
Why does the salt water need any fresh?
Much like a meeting with the wrong person,
Like kindness with no one to assess.

So, adagio, andante, neath the waves,
They run deep the orchestral vibrations,
And the lone busker's drowned out, ne'er to be saved,
For subtle and lyrical, string's tribulations.

The rain it drips on, like it would hammer on a roof
Where we would hear the songbirds' chattering,
Yet the ocean is still, quiet and aloof,
Just shimmering with sparks of sheet lightning.

One day, someone will need to come to the place
Where you're expected like one expects good tidings,
Like a stream that saves us when our thirst it slakes,
Giving us all, all of itself kindly.

Pouring forth like rain, rushing to forget
that the ocean's thirst can never be quenched
someone needs the silk thread to remain yet,
so the oceans with the sky can be drenched…

Tell me, why does the sea taste like brine
And why don't I sleep after dusk?
Why do Mum's eyes like emeralds shine
Whereas mine have a hue of rust?

Why do we value so highly the gold
That we so crave to hold in our hand,
That one day'll be just a vase, cracked and old
Discarded in a corner to stand?

What makes you venture into the deluge
With no cover above your head?
And beneath the stormy sky's plum-like hues
Dredge up old odes of deceit and dread?

Odes about love and disconnected thoughts
Inopportune and disarranged.
All your life's work is valued at nought,
And your words are held back, as if caged.

So, you'll go and remember once more
Those friends who you had once to watch leave,
You can't forget ev'rything, that's for sure —
Forgetting's not easily achieved.

But to hell with all that legacy
For there are still songs to employ.
You will give voice and there is sure to be
Something to turn you raving with joy.

And when the snowflakes fall from the sky
You'll jut your tongue like when you were small,
Brushing flakes from shoulders, you'll realise
With life there's no discontent at all.

That's when you'll recall those childhood stories,
You'll know you're not alone on this Earth,
Steps on the road return to old glories
You'll sip Beaujolais 'gain by your hearth.

You'll settle into the warmest embrace,
Forgetting all those former sorrows
A fairytale evening will then take place,
With dancing and merriment, it'll flow.

Don't be sad, it really doesn't lend
Itself, and in particular, to you.
To your frozen veranda I'll send
Some drops to treat your angina and flu,
So you suffer no more aggravation
Of boredom and melancholic blues.
All ills are oft caused by separation
And the heart being rendered in two.

My Muse flies in early in the morning,
Or when the city sleeps before dawn
She gazes but I can discern nothing.
Love or strange reproach? She won't be drawn.

Sometimes she likes to whisper quietly
As if I know nought whatsoever.
She thinks that it is easier for me
To believe we are still together.

At times with a lover's caress and tears
She asks me to believe and be brave
And that we have time and the needed years
For everything still to be saved.

I try to avoid getting all confused
And to write with a lightness of tread
And then, so proud and arrogant, my Muse
Believes we're still promised to be wed.

My character can be complicated,
I'm content in my own company.
Still, I want to believe, now I've waited
She'll fly 'gain one night to be with me.

LETUM NON OMNIA FINIT
(To Josef Brodsky)

It is sad to acknowledge that in the memory
Of folk you can remain but a random episode,
Like someone's life in yours — one of many diverse events
That roll away in the mirror that maps every
Highway in kilometre-long dotted lines, and, so I'm told,
In passing, using bridges to cross life's thread we're meant.

Bridges that link one side of the road to the other,
As if they were completely incompatible —
They are occurrences, their probability so sparse,
That crown dates, while work-worn feet from the gutter
Ask once more, why? But you're implacable —
Walking on, merely wary of dead-ends you are...

The crux of secret desires and the question
Of the meaning of life only later they'll tell.
You'll not count Via Dolorosa's ev'ry stone
And not one festive day in San-Michele...

Alma-Ata

This wonderful city remembers you and me,
Every corner here has a meaning —
Onto Lovers Boulevard from Rainy Highway
Those days and all our tender evenings

Tell me, how many days must I walk Parting Lane
To commemorative Rendezvous Square?
How dear to me these earthly thoroughfares remain
And the many days and nights, I've spent there.

In the head of the spring at the foot of the hills,
In the old park where childhood's laughter,
From the venerable old trees their dreamtime spills
Catching the beat of your heart hereafter

In its squares and gardens the chestnuts light candles
And the city will bloom once again.
The hands on our watches will whirl just like spindles;
No matter; do not fret, it's a friend.

It will all pass, my dear friend, no need to feel sad —
This city has raised us with its love
And its crossroads are sure to drive us all quite mad,
This city you and I are part of.

Loneliness it is a departing train
From a platform where there's not a soul,
And unexpectedly, like a refrain
The wind taps your back like friends of old,
Time's found to solve that eternal riddle
The recurring question, you know, why?
Answer me and don't dress as a cripple,
The queen of dilemmas; live or die?
You can spit, appalled that life's pre-ordained,
I really don't know who needs to know.
What's left is that which by the bank is claimed
Like pledged debts, you know to whom they're owed,
And does anyone care if your despair
Chaperones you to the bed where you lie.
Or happiness, like a chance bird appears
And flies through your window one fine day,
As if Ligeia Siren should find you
Floating in the warm sea, white with foam,
And sings to you her captivating tune
Luring you to her, as if to home.
And she entreats you to hope for the best,
The best is yet to come she assures.
You believe her and, in a flash or less,
She's waiting for you there on the shore.
Pack your things, for the magazine is primed
All's been measured and time's all but spent
Here's the offer — another life sublime
While you still have your drive and your strength.
Believe in God or not as you incline,
But God, He awaits you and your tale,
It's better to measure a seventh time,
And make the cut just once or else fail.
And how perfect it is, our loneliness,
For it cuts through meaning like a blade
You're wonderful, Loneliness, Your Highness,
But nought from you, Siren, to be said…

Nocturne

Into my pages, quite like sand
Have been poured
From a ewer in the hand
All the words
But it seems you have watered
wrong flowers —
All those weeds and the spearwort
and sticks showered.
The river of life has dragged
The bell-shaped heart.
And the stems they are now snagged,
Trailed over rocks from afar,
Twas music that gave me light,
Calling true,
Over the keys in the night,
All was blue.
My head spun, in the wind dipped,
Biting, ill-meant
Words that were blown from my lips —
Will they ever be silent?
I'll try to put myself now
Together again,
From recollections, and doing so
I will live,
In fallen note tentative,
A silent refrain,
That pearl of music your sensitive
Fingers play.

Liberamente *

My youngest son is of Christ's age these days
I envy him. Not jealously, rather like a friend
His freedom innate, simple in its ways,
Is serious and pure from beginning to its end.
Standing on the threshold he waves goodbye
But I'm happy — in him I see my own soul,
Like I am his associate and close ally;
I so want to journey with him cheek by jowl.
Let your life be wonderful and beautiful,
Liberamente in rhyme and reason.
My eldest son, it's me and you of late,
We sail like ships bound on different courses,
As if Peter's bridges we navigate,
At night we part, our hands once joined, now divorced.
But your path is hard, the channel is deep
how many eyes are riveted tight on you,
The truths you face are ever higher, steep;
Let those who will listen, hear your voice as true.
Let your life be wonderful and beautiful,
Liberamente in rhyme and reason.
Life is hard and its circle on my keys,
The circle of joy and pain holding sway,
And I will always be lacking the notes
With which you depart to climes far away.
Meanwhile, though, life is wonderful and beautiful,
Liberamente in rhyme and reason...

* Liberamente – Italian musical term for "freely"
** Peter — Saint-Petersburg

Penelope

I know it, oh I know it well,
Old age weeps meek for you on the side,
I know, oh I know well, you can't exist
With all in perfect harmony,
Your fate, like Odysseus, ne'er to dwell,
Could someone who in youth resides?
Or would fatigue never you resist?
Just don't you forget about me.

I can see that wild youth rising,
Dancing in your hotly beating heart,
And I know, if there's another way,
Life a shadow on the wall will be.
There are folk in whom the striving
To sing has awoken with a start
The heart'll speak love for things prosaic
If only there's a line for me.

I believe, I do, that it'll cease,
And sadness will turn another page
And battles with the right blood hereof
Will comfort the world, then you'll see:
You'll return, we'll all have release,
At the threshold that's waited an age
You'll recall my reason with but love
And with it, you'll recognise me…

Memory...

Upon happy Junes, Februaries
Memory looks with forgotten gaze;
Rain-washed and happy memories
And half-remembered nights and days.
Hopes smashed to pieces on the road,
And however hard you cry and weep,
Pages in smart books forever closed
Remaining silent as you sleep.

Like a bird life it has flown by
And out there on the wing somewhere
Is silted up, a river now dry —
You'd hesitate to twice enter there.
The belated embraces
Turned cold like tea that's now chilled,
And gazing into tired faces,
You quietly say farewell; and still

Memory with cobwebs of gold
is woven and on the wind borne,
Mute clouds that melt away untold
With each returning dawn.

Waiting is adulthood,
About the torrential rain,
About despair, the abyss underfoot,
About "don't know what there's to gain".

Waiting's for hale and hearty,
Undiluted, quiet in the night
Sky it adds hues of navy partly
Then colours of azure more light.

It is the air which is insufficient,
And water enough for one sip,
It is the morning that's still distant,
And the candle's smouldering tip.

Waiting — it is not for a bus,
For really, it's a matter of years.
Perhaps it's the thing that is saving us
And keeping it spinning, the Earth's sphere...

Minutes, hours and days of our lives

They depart like into the mountains depart
Our dearest friends, who are to return here no more,
As they go, like quiet stream, so goes their fracas
About the things that will and will not lie in store.

Later they won't recall who left whom behind
And how many meetings postponed till late.
So, why did we need so many words and rules assigned,
Smart formulae just to obliterate

The memory of what linked us with this earth so warm
Holding the firmament as if in spiders' threads,
And chiming each spring like a young brass orchestra formed.
The sky it hung suspended like a quilted plaid.

Chiming about how poplar-made pyramids
Decorate the spring in sticky new leaves and then,
Like a female hand waves, wishing farewell to us bid,
Sadness of days gone trembles as
through days it wends.

Brodsky, he reads Pushkin, the tone
Rather flat, a bit stuttering.
As he has plenty of his own,
Why does he need to be struggling?

Brodsky, for the US it's not strenuous,
The Nobel Prize can't be bought for a cent,
I think; what it really needs from us
Is Pushkin's *Wondrous Moment*.

In Washington, dear Brodsky, Pushkin
Has mudslingers few and far between,
And not in Yiddish, English nor Pashtu,
But in his very own Russian seen.

All the greats have to go and Brodsky's no more,
Time is dust, but with light of encouragement,
A word alone can deformity cure,
A word alone can truly gift a moment.

Sitting and listening, those who can hear,
Leaping across the centuries,
Poets, they give something personal, dear
From their distant far distances.

Kintsugi*

Like everything around us, I remind,
We are prone to breaking and cracking,
And the cracks can be so cruel and unseemly
To us and our fates, perhaps many times.
We're destined always to be tracking
Sadly within the cracks that are seen and
Within those hidden away deeply.

Trying to still the pain, the meaning sour, secret,
We strive at times to hide it and perhaps forget it too
Just as if we were to forget our failings,
And, in the meantime, the thought we reject:
To be a proper person through and through
The lessons we've learned should ere be prevailing.

Of course, it's hard to believe and to continue
Filling a cracked vessel with newly found
Exhilaration,
And yet life always gives us the strength to renew,
Rise from the ashes and ruins,
At journey's end to *judicum dei* bound
Pockmarked by inclement precipitation.

You see, this is our life.
It's inseparable from us.
Life's record.
This is us.

---

* *Kintsugi* is the Japanese art of repairing broken pottery by
mending the areas of breakage with *urushi* lacquer dusted or
mixed with powdered gold, silver, or platinum. The philosophy
behind this art form is that breakages and cracks are an integral
part of the object's history and, therefore, should not be neglected
or masked.

You suddenly realize on the footplate,
Soft rocking you in the swell,
You're riding on the tramcar of your fate.
Rushing headlong to the depths of Hell,

Through a landscape of concrete and glass,
Neon nights hold in captivity,
Partings and meets like a marathon pass
To wordless commonality.

Some people want to remain impassive,
Preferring quiet and peace
And float to all that's inexpressive
Pretending at times to be grass.

And those from whom, like a lava flow,
Passion and blood come in a rush
Value the moment, the to and the fro,
For vibrant life and love aren't frivolous.

And they fly like a flaming comet
Past those who shiver from fear,
For that tram won't fly like a rocket
To the light; there's no stopping it here.

Past those who are living in mousetraps,
Drinking tea that's long since gone cold
Living out their lives at the tram stops
Where the solid ground takes hold…

Clouds

They married us, married us away
Did those fluffy clouds that floated by
They seemed to drift by, carefree that day,
Just looking on down from way up high.

But once they looked down sly, like on prey
As if joking but with a crafty eye
They married us, married us away
Did those fluffy clouds that floated by.

We weren't expecting and couldn't say,
But into one hand another complied,
They married us, married us away
Did those fluffy clouds that floated by.

Love from the heavens to us gave they,
The river it is full of the sky;
They too were clearly in love, I'd say,
Those fluffy clouds that floated on by.

Autumn plays its tricks again,
Weaving a leafy cloak.
Rain will trickle down the panes
Leaving a trail with its strokes.

Who told you that you'd be blue
And that a tear by chance will fall?
No, autumn will come, bringing you
Strong tea when it comes to call.

Don't go regretting the summer,
It will return again.
Autumn shimmers for all comers
Rushing to embrace and ken.

She too is a guest no more, it's said,
And rushes here to explain
That life is vast, yet finer thread
Than spider's web contains.

Angel

An angel's popped in for a chat
And a nice cup of tea.
It's spread its wings out on the mat.
So they don't get crumpled, you see.

It's rather cramped in the kitchen,
It's not easy with wings.
But we're having a lovely time
With buns and pies and things.

He really is so busy
Flying from here and to there,
There are times, however, when he
Would like earthly joy to share.

Here sits this fine young fellow,
I've known him a long time.
He's most kind and really smart, you know,
An angel talented, in his prime.

With him I always feel younger,
And much like him I try to be.
I chat as I wish and no wonder,
With him as your friend, you'd agree.

I'd ask him to stay — that's absurd,
For their call I hear from the sky.
And waving his wings like a bird,
Away to the clouds he does fly.

The Autumn of My Grief...

Someone likes poems to read,
Another, at night writes leaves
And yellowing, in flight they lead
To the autumn of my grief.

Oh, Autumn, how many songs
Have been sung to you, yet still you're sad.
Shall I add one to the throng?
No? Well, I'm singing it all the same.

You're clearly so clouded and dull and
To all of this vast human race,
That all your verses are so sullen
Well, there's much sullenness to embrace.

Maybe that's enough, my dear!
Why not caress me with a sunny day?
I'll not be writing more songs this year;
You're too cold so I'll wait for next May.

What am I to do? For on the long road
I have lost my friends on the way,
And all of that pain and worry's load
Are still walking with me today.

You alone are my true companion,
Very kind and so funny at times,
You warm when its cold, shedding your light on
My way — you're always by my side.

What will my soul have to pay tomorrow
For the warmth of your evening's fire,
When the sun it rolls its disk so low
Till morning deep into the mire?

How can I ever repay you, my dear
For a water's sip in the heat?
I simply cannot figure out, why we're
Ever joined as in one heartbeat.

I walk on, there's still a long way for me,
I'll surely pay you back in kind.
At night I'll spread a stars' canopy
At noon offer shade when inclined.

And although it's often not that painless —
You see that no angel am I —
You'll not be forgotten, you know this,
By this loving soul of mine.

I'll give you a sunset's blazing red glow,
I'll give to you blue oceans fine,
You'll never be forgotten, so you know,
By this loving soul of mine!

Have you tried to meet with your memory
And with your cards on the table commune,
Without accusation, anger, injury,
And not be to others' kindness immune?
Testing questions, there may be a multitude
To the pendulum's slow swing in the calm,
Like watery droplets that find their way, you'd
Witness answers without falsehoods to harm.
Have you tried staring into the looking glass,
Calmly, with no hint of passion or shame,
To see from the deep pool with swirls
of quicksilver amassed
Another stares back at you through the frame?
And that gaze, so silent and cautious, will hint,
That, as if straight from an Internet page,
Our earthly path is a wondrous labyrinth —
You'll need to walk on 'neath conscience's gaze.
Have you tried listening to how your own voice sounds?
The pitch, is it right, the tone and all that?
You might then realise that you should turn it down,
To hear then what others might wish to add.
Have you tried to remember your encounters?
The ones that conjure memories most true,
When the magic was like snow on your shoulders,
Like solid white in the heavenly blue...

There is a beautiful woman,
Her fortieth year gone by,
She might weep at times, much like autumn,
At times like sunrise is nigh.

She can have blizzards, with both ice and snow,
The desert's sultry heat,
Shoulders that in the morning do glow
With cool freshness sweet.

There is a beautiful woman,
Her fortieth year gone by,
To whom both tender light and hope can
Attract so irresistibly.

In her there is birth and aspiration,
first words a child will say,
And then a day of desperation
Yet a night like fragrant hay.

Her years pass by so noiselessly
Like silent movies of old,
Mundane, yet mercilessly
The countdown continues to roll.

Time walks beside her, its gait
Light, as she departs away.
Tender music creates
A mood to keep grief at bay…

New Year, Parting Year...

We'll see in the New, of course we will,
It'll be coming home all the same.
Each guest we'll welcome, keep glasses filled
A heartfelt "Salut!" we will proclaim.

I cannot say that I know this New Year,
Or if it is something I'm up to,
Rather than greeting the season with cheer,
A send-off for the parting I'd do.

He who wants to go, let him up and leave,
I'll not hold back those departing,
My heart will see him off, I won't grieve,
With a smile tell him don't be hurting.

He will leave and his last breath he will take
Of that December as it goes.
In pyramids the street cleaner does make
The last calendar's files out of snow.

You don't have to look over your shoulder,
You'll find no answers in what's gone,
New Year, be kind to me, not colder,
While I hit Delete on what's done.

Come now, it's time to wake up, my darling,
My sleeping beauty, that you are.
I know how you like our room so charming,
For simplicity you need not look far.
While the noise just sighs outside our window,
While the sunlight a little it glides,
It is easier for the heart to count down
The seconds — in tender song they hide.
We can fail sometimes each other to hear,
On occasion we don't seek with our eyes.
Despite endeavour, mistakes can appear,
And sadness at home can arise.
Perhaps it is down to our life's prose,
The fault of that curséd bitter salt,
It turns out, this splinter it grows and grows,
With persistent sharp pain to assault.
May all foul weather simply drift on by,
I'm not counting the years but the days.
I'll buy harbours of ships and aeroplanes for the skies,
Let's do away with all this, just say…
Then snippets of bright-coloured sunsets,
Exotic hops, tattoos I'll buy too,
You'll see it all as a chore to get,
But I'm happy giving all to you.
Don't be forlorn, for no furious gale
Will extinguish that fire inside me,
There'll be evening after the day's travail,
Tenderness and a nice cup of tea…

What I remember of this evening,
What gave solace to my sorrow,
Like fatigue on shoulders, reclining
The slanting rain on my window.

I remembered something dear to me
Not to everyone I can expound.
Evening whispers but only simply,
Simple words they cannot be found.

And so a secret let it remain,
Myself, I'll forget it for sure,
Not for long, just till, by chance, again,
I return to familiar door.

Promise not to miss me, not weep or sob,
From your window not gaze with yearning,
The rain will fall as your tears to drop
All the same from the early morning.

And when you notice in the autumn breeze
The intertwining of leafy bouquets,
Realise how worthy you are, please,
This autumn, this day and you of praise.

The Birthday

Approximately fourteen minutes,
Fifteen perhaps,
I'll smoke my cigarette, curse midnight rain,
And then at twelve,
Like an old shutter claps,
The hands will wipe yet another year for my pain.

Oh, let it ride,
Just a number are my years,
And if at basic sums I were stronger
I would prefer that the meaning be clear:
That the total sum of life were longer.

Into the world did this scallywag come,
I'd like to embrace you all and expound,
A birthday's not a gala, but a reason
To remember one, another discount…

Sleep's like a little death and I'm dying,
But, knowing it is just a chasm between,
It leaves aroma of orange and peel trying,
To set down the line between me and my dreams.

The dawn, as if hungover and straining,
Will endeavour to connect the day before
With the new, while the enduring meaning
Of life will catch within the snags like a lure.

I hope my heartbeat won't suffer a lull
Sickly like when I was a boy,
Like a pause between scenes, an interval,
Of inaction interspersed with joy

Like Groundhog Day it repeats,
Make good, discover your way to the temple,
For the morning will bring the heat
For what's been said or unsaid. It's simple:

The drama of the past can ne'er be healed.
It may appear but may not even seem real
For not everyone will believe
That love and oppression may be two halves
revealed.

Where the world hangs by a spider's thread,
Sleep is not a burden, but bliss
Feel the contented solitude of bed
While the Moon drops to the sea with a kiss.

It's easy to see smiles on tired faces
Of old friends who have now gone away,
Perhaps just for vodka, or distant places,
And not be recognising them today.
Shielded from worries by the rain as it pours
And alien, unfamiliar, office doors,
Those once with you are no longer by your side
And in the zebra on the tarmac wide,
Floating away twixt changing traffic signal
There flashes a face, then a lodging; you recall
Dull echoes of half-empty spaces — after,
You hear notes and the fragments of laughter.
That parquet floorboard, oh-so guiltily stained!
With some of that cheap and nasty Bordeaux
That the old landlady has not rubbed away
And in the size of a birthmark it's soaked.
Love or friendship, it's not now quite as bright
And smoke — the kind you no longer breathe,
You don't smoke, almost don't drink out of spite,
You can't make it out, not all's to see.
But it's turned green and the zebra's now away,
Lamplight distantly shuddered, froze and out it went;
Out there awaits with malicious intent,
That which shivered in the light the previous day…

Is time really so omnipotent
To each of us measure in years,
And in misfortune so abundant
Our path as if in rain to veneer?
Placing my trust not only in reason
On my way I continued to tread.
I made way for a random rideshare on
The road, and as I strode ahead,
I came across a coppice so curly
Like that Rita, so long ago,
At that school of ours with the number three
On Kirova, by the picturedome.
There was nothing going on between us
To suddenly recall her name.
Rita, no more are those pals from our class,
Chernobyl or the booze to blame.
You might now be in Tel Aviv living,
A most troubled place, do believe me:
Those who upped sticks to be travelling
There now call me and cite misery.
Once the battle was fought for reds or whites,
But now just try and work it out,
The day begins and all's clear and bright
But by evening, hold on to your hat.
But you need to keep going, that's cherished,
"Rolling stones they gather…" you know
What I mean, and we'll ne'er see replenished
Again, those golden times of old.
There's no further need for us to count down,
The years, for they can scream for themselves;
To questions, the muddy waters brown
Of the Jordan have nought to tell…
The waves' dull whispering
And the chatter of the trees

Entered my home at night without invite.
My glass brimming
I harked that absurdity,
Writing poems, trusting in candlelight.
My inks out I spread
On narrow streaks of light,
And maybe drew the morning's dawn nearer,
Who's been tormented
By that sweetness at night
Might now understand me that much clearer.
It was far from dull
For the stars, like little birdies,
Flocked together by my open window,
Where I sat enthralled.
From my page these sweeties
I fed with lines, and light the darkness did swallow.
A simple affair,
For to give was so nice
And resign to the sweetest confinement —
A tender isle where
My soul in but a trice
Forgot ev'rything, no return was meant
Nor was it asking.
On such nights might Petrarch
To his belovéd Laura be writing?
The night was passing,
It was hot and my heart
Ached and meantime
Quiet moon was reclining…

Farewell, city,
Thank you for the light,
Chance warmth — pity,
It's now taken flight.
In fierce-cold days with
An echo around,
A dead gesture stiff
In limp hands found.
Weather-stained evening
In cloudy night sky,
Verandah, wind keening,
A hasty love's try,
A touching of lips,
Then in retort,
A snowstorm takes grip,
Lump in the throat.
A memento is left
In hand's tight clasp,
On a hair's breadth turns deft,
Looks back to glance.
From an unspoken word,
From sounded riposte,
A thing that's straightforward,
Now forever lost…

Not to a church, a mosque or a synagogue,
Will I ever my soul be steering,
At night I will pray quietly to god
While at a wonderful star peering,
The star that illuminates my journey
While the dark night embraces this globe,
At night I will pray to god serenely,
Ask that others and that star have hope.
I'll ask to help the traveller feel better,
For in parting too grave was their sigh,
So the burden won't weigh on their shoulders,
And the thunder's loud clap won't surprise.
I'll pray for those close by and more distant,
For my acquaintances and my friends,
Those with goodness and sentiment blessed and,
My relatives and my children.
I will pray for women, kind and gentle,
Who live with others in happiness,
Let wanderers midst the snowstorms settle,
In salvatory shelter find rest.
And let the years be like an open book
Telling how sweet this life we lead,
And of course, nor love will they overlook
Nor the happiness that love doth feed.
That wonderful star — it's an offering from god,
The star that holds me firm on the edge,
The star that lights my way from the threshold
The far from simple life of this wretch…

A Dream / Pygmalion 2 /

I made her up, or just saw her in my head,
It might've been a dream, perhaps a game,
A hundred hues, a hundred shades spread
When morning came,
I'd created her, unequivocal,
And I drew her,
In colour in a perfect charcoal oval:
red, green and ochre,
A low voice too, the kind I love — in full bloom,
Well-shaped,
With lips like petals of the field, in perfumed
Thornapple draped.
Then to the clouds I set her free; till mute stars had burned
And could burn no more, until colours soft
Had all washed away on the rain, I observed
Her gently waft…

On one of these days I want walking to go
Counting off the steps with the pulse
In my veins,
Like trudging ever wearier up a mountain track
And with my dearest by my side, I shall go
To find the fine lace of thought in
me contained.
With no conversation to distract,
So empty in this false and silent place,
A silence granted like a gift from the gods,
Like a woman who loves but holds her peace
And of those awkward things not speculate,
Reminding me how many poor steps I've trod,
With that lonely desperate heart the beats increase.
Silence watches over things which must not be said
It hangs easier than dew upon the pines
And how can I not shout with joy from the peaks.
I do not count how many of my years have fled
On a beam, horizon's blue edge defines
Like the jagged cliffs, my eyes are wrinkle-streaked
On one of these days, I want to fly
Escaping earth's clinging gravity,
In a wicked, haughty stepmother's cold grasp that's held.
And with sharp carving of ski on ice
Earth's umbilical's cut and free.
With protracted melody these unkind hills
Devour themselves,
But for now, there is a time for other places —
It's not yet for me to gift my fatal embraces.

You and I are Different

(in response to Marina Tsvetaeva)

"...We differ, yes we do. Verily a blessing!
And we complement each other well,
What can such similarity be expressing?
Just a vicious-circle it doth foretell."

Our difference has different things in store
For us — delight of knowledge, joy of meeting,
At times we'll misunderstand each other for sure
But similarity
Might lose from a word fleeting...

The Centaur

Someone measures their path lengthwise,
And the hours vertically,
Add booze to the minor key and, surprise!
A seesaw not scales you'll see.

'bout love no more do I want to sing,
There's simply nothing I can explain,
When it's hard to breathe, don't be rending
Apart Ariadne's tangled yarn.

Like ice from a breaker letters cast,
And so they would finally come clear,
I tossed them into lines of verse, thinking it'd pass,
And no one would think me a liar.

It's time to admit — I'm a centaur.
Oh, Cronos and Mother Filly,
Where to find the triumphal laurel?
The steppe stands smoking before me.

Where will you run from your fate in the end,
With fatal poison your wound laced?
By the cold arrow of a true friend
Back to mortal ranks I'll race.

But while hooves beat their triumphant march on
the drums
of the Earth
Orpheus sings,
The centaurs, fatefully but fervently, come
The sweet river of their lives to drink…

Humanity, it resides in me,
Lulling to sleep when moon is full.
Come morning, like in insanity,
It incinerates as to flames it pulls.

Humanity is Schnitke, Mozart
And the dombra's heartfelt refrain.
Despite the torture and tearing apart,
Don't capitulate, defy the pain!

Humanity is Brodsky, Abai,
Akhmatova, Blok and Shakespeare.
Humanity is, like as an orphan I
From neath kind yet tearful lines do peer.

Humanity, it's feeling unease
Midst cataclysms and the anger of waves.
Our tears they fall saltier than seas:
Why does our god from wars not save?

Humanity is you and me,
Might now be the time to make
The world much kinder for everybody,
In words and deeds, for our sakes.

But we won't manage, for the wind it will
Through its mesh riddle our teary vale.
Words in granite across it will fill
And tears of salt will trail.

Coloured in chalky white
The city slept
And a smart old man with dangling legs
On a cloud fluffy, light,
Nonchalantly swept
Below onto the road the snow's dregs.

Fir tree with halo,
On windowpanes silver —
The words they transform to vapour,
Like those Tarot
Cards in noir familiar,
Scrawling notes to strangers.

New Year comes as a shock,
A stranger arriving,
Slowly and just like back when
The hand on the wall clock
Will be turning
The calendar's last page again.

Like customary nights,
We, much the same
Will imbibe those heady hopes,
A flute raise we might
Full of what's not ours to name,
that'll melt away at dawn like smoke…

Somewhere birthdays are left in the wake,
Back in childhood, in the dawn sun.
Expectation of joy and summer breaks,
For the time being, time has moved on…

With the passing years there's confusion
On this day of whim and caprice,
Life should be a stairway's ascension
But sometimes down the pole of grease.

And there's no need to be spurring us on,
Any brakes would only suppress,
And in the mirror those wrinkles conjoin
Beneath eyes that are quite helpless.

Each day, in criss-cross fashion, the board
Arrivals and departures displays.
Where days as a matter of minutes are stored
Or from spite pour into rivers away.

This day contains a meeting, a gift —
A coffee served with kindly eyes,
Only your world is to be short-lived,
Like your character and your rites.

Where a standard comma grows, reaching
The size of a dash or a hyphen,
I close my eyes as I'm flying, leaving,
To pages struck through one by one.

Time is beating on ice between the lines
About love and it is wonderful,
But in the ellipsis spaces you'll find
It's like February — cold, miserable…

Don't you trouble me, just don't you dare,
To be drowning in doubt I'm not needing.
After all, I can breathe no more lies where
Sun's rays through the murk won't be bleeding.

Don't you trouble me, just set me free
Let me simmer down, recollection,
Where surf hits land, where you won't find me,
Nor will grief nor other affliction.

Don't trouble me, on Earth I'm seeking
A Garden of Eden, my stresses
To forget, then sleep, like a droplet lingering
On shard ere it slides to the abyss…

Our language with words is packed
But the one I need can't be found,
Like needle in a haystack
Or the end of the earth's track —
I see, but it still confounds.

When you take that arm of mine
Your sweet curls fall in sighs
And my gaze cannot untwine,
Like a New Year outfit fine
The flames that burn in your eyes.

Time, it steals nights when we dream,
Time, it's like water flowing,
By the by, away it teems,
Life ebbs like a polluted stream,
Not knowing where it's going.

I stick again at my quest
For words, again and again,
As if another to wrest
Unearthly recognition blessed,
And my thoughts' bowstring does strain.

It's good that you're reticent
In words you see nought righteous.
Yes, spring it was impatient,
Summer — hot, intolerant;
Autumn now be bounteous…

On and on the sea grinds,
Wordless, jaded,
No intonation, not a trace.
I felt aggrieved,
In fact astounded —
The waves' notes crash
Quite devoid of grace.

Like in a hammock down below,
The splashing water lulls me to sleep,
Carrying away to frescoes yellow,
From everything far away to keep.

Instinctively, we want the sea, at least
A sight of that sea, but not I —
The thing on which my eyes would feast
Are the vast steppes and mountains high.

I cannot sleep to old masts creaking
Nor under the yard arm dream.
I'd like a fractured contour, sweeping
Where from steppes mountains rise supreme.

Where fragrant allium's most piquant and
Burial mounds thousand-year secrets watch,
The wormwood, sagebrush and tulips fan
The night just like the sea, its light and cobalt…

I need to go see my dad
Also see my ma
Go to the churchyard
To pray, lay a wreath with flowers clad,

Whispering through the headstones of granite,
While the blinding deluge falls like tears
And patters, the heat of grave slabs abates
One summer's day and, as I disappear,

Say that I do not know how much more
I'll be interested in living,
That my Polish angel I adore
Prevents my days from shivering,

That I write about various things,
In words, maybe, far from simple,
And I appear indolent, I think
And for my age seem quite nimble.

It often seems most peculiar
That life's like a spiral's steep state.
I'm driven to countries near and far
But there endure an orphan's fate.

I'll ask them to manifest patience
Before the funeral feast is here;
I'll ask for inspiration, hesitance
And a love for this life so dear...

A thought about a lost paradise —
I store, not like stuff from old times,
But in me like a forgotten place
That forgotten happiness of mine.
Embroidery on an old garment
Stitched in a thread that's so fine
A postcard patch, like a fragment
That forgotten happiness of mine.
To the drips of the clock on the wall
On its chain, drops form from the roof,
Long-forgotten April baulks
And sings, so as not to be aloof.
Is it childhood, youth, maturity?
Beyond mountain, river, vanishing point
Where it's all s'posed to have surety
Is sewn with an invisible joint.
And this is still not a refrain
That song's still not unveiled
The cup is still heavy and strained
That ship has still far to sail.
In springtime the tall pines they weep
Tears of almost Baltic-like amber,
My forgotten reveries run deep
Under grey rain, 'til September.
When it's dry in that forgotten room
The cosmos takes aim through the chink
The grass exudes a heady perfume
And a fly my bed's warmth will drink.

I'm in two minds 'bout moving,
The hay breathes like poison, sweet
I labour for air, heaving
Time into its funnel retreats.

Kitbuqa*

I'm writing verses,
Don't you seek my descendants,
Not anywhere will you now find.
You think my voice is
For earthly elements
Slight? In water I write my lines.
Once a vision I had:
My forefathers sped
On horseback age after age
Ringing sabres clad,
Mothers weep with dread,
In blood to the land paid homage.
Our blood it spilled over
And you won't find the shores,
Past the Danube, in Balkan gardens,
On rocks in Syria,
Age after age and more,
It rises in colours that redden.
Our blood it boiled over
In heaven's cauldrons,
On fires of Siberia's taiga.
Above Naiman** banners were
Troops Lithuanian
Proudly flying our coats of arms.
How many women lovely,
Like ripest fruits
Are we to sample as we trek on?
We took keys to cities,
And we took this tribute,
And plenty of wine and locum.
Beijing and Damascus,

The Yellow Sea's poison,
And a rare glimpse back of Altai,
Heavenward we rushed
To the annals and on
Chasing others' dreams to hell fly.
How did I then survive?
Or remain alive?
Let them hear me everywhere,
The water in our blood has long since
vaporised!
You think it's in water I scribe?
I remained alive
With a sword's sliver,
Now thrills of it through my veins course,
Nothing can I imbibe,
Kitbuqa stands hither,
Waiting for me to saddle my horse.
The water may chime
And sing in the creek
Or it may in the pond quiet grieve.
It may hark words of mine
That I want to speak
And retell them to those it receives.

* Kitbuqa is a historical figure from the 13th century
Mongol Empire
** The Naimans are one of the historical clans of the
Kazakhs

My Dream smiled at the threshold, and then she took flight,
Leaving me not even a shadow.
Should I have pursued, o'er deceitful roads, that night?
If only I'd known where to follow.

I would have run, but my
envy of the world's passed.
These lips don't ask for water my thirst
to slake; these feet have long since forgotten the grass,
My mem'ry — the shards when a star bursts.

With what in myself winter's breath do I gauge?
Mercury shivers and falls.
You believe the mute numbers —
your passport age?
Temples ache, like snow in a squall.

I asked the sky and the reply to my request:
The web of years yourself consult.
You've walked a hundred roads, scattering your missteps
Countless questions but no result.

But my Dream, deep in thought, keeps count, as I
Stand speechless like dust at one's feet,
We'll keep silent and let the river surge on by,
She'll know my threshold where to meet.

There in my solitude where
Every thought is half-undressed,
Autumn's beyond the window there,
I'm living like summer blessed.
Let autumn and then winter cold
Continue to weep quietly,
Meantime sadness and rain, behold —
Drip to slush compliantly.
Once spring comes, there'll not be much chance
That someone will ever hark,
Flames at sunrise on roofs will dance
Like pan lids on fiery sparks.
'cross March, its bridges in between,
In a crowd and barely clothed,
I'll cover shrubs with brush of green
To get the summer exposed.

I talk to myself from time to time
And sometimes with you but not often,
Like at nighttime a wall white primed,
Glows bright as my *I* speaks with me and,
In response, avoiding the light,
Your own *You* an answer returns me,
Failing to recognise my right
To an answer, speaking non-verbally.
There are 'whats' and 'what fors' aplenty;
The thing I need from myself and from you
floats into darkness, silent, empty —
Just a line of words that obeys the mood.
And they're not about that, those woes,
Nor 'bout those who will one day betray.
It's just that later this will be posed,
Quite possibly twice and what we say
Should be exclusively good and kind;
Made a mistake but all was excused,
To you just an aching head consigned.
Well, an ache is all it could be infused
With, when so many questions amass
Like a dark cloud hanging low in the sky,
Grey, overcast and drizzle's forecast
We're far from the meaning, can't deny,
All life's meanings and those of death too,
These secrets and Heaven's Seven Seals.
God spoke, believe it or not's up to you,
We wait for God's grace to reveal…

December, Terrainkur*

When December's joyously sprinkling
Its confetti from snow-decked fir trees,
We will just forget we were so missing the spring,
And we'll surely remember our youth
With glee.
And here, topped with a fine coating of ice,
The river says to us what we can't make out,
But all the same we understand most precise —
With December of the same thing they shout.
Water that can talk — can you just imagine —
Well, why then does that not make it human?
Raise its voice a little, what'll happen?
Wires will drop their arms and snow will loosen.
After that there will be a little more snow,
A gift from one of generous spirit.
That snow wishes cleanliness from the sky
To bestow
And falls silently like a shawl knitted.
Please, December, take your time, I ask,
Don't be rushing to turn your pages;
Let your nighttime floorboards creak in many places,
To sing in the night's silence, the stream's task.

*Methodical movement of the body on ascending terrain
for healing purposes

So, New Year, we come to you
But you're not new,
Thankfully, you're able
To accept
At times, like ace of clubs,
Hot-headed were you,
You burned bridges so as not to remember, yet
Whatever it may be, you have to go through it,
Through that thing that has been labelled fate,
You might not half the journey revisit
But out there half the journey still awaits,
Unforeseeably and fabulously revealed —
The thirtieth day's threshold delivered
When Hoffmann's tale comes and to all it will appeal,
Nutcracker and Marie, and into the mirrors
The sugarplum fairy will view her reflection
But that is not what dreams really concern,
When between snow-covered crowns, decoration
So bright; New Year comes and with it return
Our hopes that are dark, unclear and unconscious,
like in childhood, little known, randomly,
you'll enjoy the bustle just like before this
and you'll barely notice it's time for tea.
But still you want to enjoy your fantasy,
New, of course, the old one's for the dumper;
You'll have to choose between those and these,
Many miles from December to summer.
In this life may God good fortune grant to you,
Like Chance, that fortune is God's alias,
So, don't think you can't see, for both good fortune
And chance are blood brothers with happiness.
And what is New Year for you prophesying,

What'll it be like, hoisted aloft, your flag?
Let December be itself applying,
Looking in its deep old chest for
Cognac...

A fond farewell, this autumn's last evening,
How mournful your November overtones,
Air's membrane breathes a barely perceptible moan
Through the noise of cars and distant barking —
In minor key nature gave its salute:
A nod to nonchalance,
Warmth's price is free gratis.
It froze stock still, in its full birthday suit
With a lilac bush transformed to dry switch.
Everything's so familiar, almost routine,
No one weeps, just the rain outside the window pane
In shy, streaking droplets, forms a picture to be seen,
Steadily pondering one thing to ascertain,
That life is characterised by frailty,
With spiralling nature, changing scenery.
The time has come to show some humility,
No words, sighs, ovations unnecessary.
Like a text: you get it, add a bracket grin,
A sticker, and slowly to coat from jacket;
Tomorrow on speaker, today receiving —
Today it's this, tomorrow will be that,
A good thing there are no limits for a word
That strides on through inclement weather,
Advancing from London, Paris, undeterred,
Over and over and flagging never.
That's what will always keep you cosy and warm,
Spending time with only those who understand,
So let the rain turn a little white by dawn
As like words onto your paper it lands...